Alcoholism & Addiction AA Recovery Handbook

How To Write A Fourth Step As The Key To Recovery For The Alcoholic & Addict

A Recovery and Development Publication

Alcoholism & Addiction AA Recovery Handbook
How To Write A Fourth Step As The Key To Recovery For The Alcoholic & Addict

Over many years the twelve step program of recovery has expanded its influence.

Originally intended to help alcoholics, 12-step recovery has broadened its application to address many other addictions and phenomena. In fact, the book *Alcoholics Anonymous* indicates that the way of life it describes offers benefits for all.

This handbook is designed to assist you in developing a fulfilling and durable recovery experience which you can then pass on to others. Admittedly, what it describes is hard work and requires commitment, but rest assured that the efforts that one puts into this work will be multiplied with the rewards of a good life.

1. Table of Contents

2. Introduction

Alcoholism & Addiction AA Recovery Handbook is a supplemental guide to the fourth step instructions found in the book *Alcoholics Anonymous* (the Big Book)[1].

It is designed for all people involved in any 12-step recovery program including newcomers, others who may want to improve the quality of their recovery, and any sponsor wishing to be helpful.

Step four itself is a key milestone in recovery, while steps 5, 8, 9, 10, and 12 additionally rely directly upon the successful completion of a fourth step inventory.

> **Step 5:** We read our 4th step to a trusted person in step 5.
> **Step 8:** Step four provides the eighth step amends list.
> **Step 9:** This amends list allows us to make amends in step 9.
> **Step 10:** We continue our inventory process in step 10.
> **Step 12:** We transmit this understanding to others in step 12.

Although each personal inventory is unique, the process, concepts, and templates are common to all.

This guide provides clear examples on how to write an efficient and complete fourth step inventory to help ensure quality sobriety and the clarity to then be helpful to others.

---

[1] This guide is non-conference approved literature and is meant to supplement the Big Book. It is based on personal experience with recovery and only discusses those steps which rely directly upon step four. Of course all 12 steps are vital and should be worked with a sponsor whenever possible.

3. Fourth Step Overview

3.1. Notes

We regularly ask for God's help during this process.

- Having completed steps one, two, and three, we are open to God's help.
- God provides the strength to move steadily through this work.

Inventory helps us rely on God.

- It reveals that we can't live successfully based on our finite selves.
- Inventory does not provide mastery and self-management of thoughts, feelings, and actions - remember, self-knowledge alone avails us nothing.
- Ultimately we are not able to wish away our character defects any more than we can our disease or dysfunction, even when we understand them, without God's help.
- We therefore need and turn to God - this is the ultimate purpose of step 4.

It's recommended we work with a sponsor.

- This allows us to discuss our progress, experience, and any questions which may arise.

Step four is a fact-finding process.

- We are not indulging feelings, purging emotions, or writing a novel.
- We simply review our lives within the inventory templates as they are designed.
- All inventories are unique, however, the templates and concepts are common to all.

We hand write inventory.

- Learning to organize handwritten inventory in notebooks teaches us how to pass this experience on to others.
- Using a computer is not recommended. (This removes the possibility of losing the entire body of work due to unexpected equipment failure, or unwanted intrusion, etc.)
- The simple hand-written practice in step four helps us continue written inventory in step ten.
- Writing on only one side of the pages makes the work more legible when we read the material in step 5 or share samples in step 12.

Step four typically takes from six months to a year to complete.

- This estimate depends on our dedication and the extent of our inventory; the depth of our handicaps, and our quantity of experience.

Step four is a finite endeavor.

- A successful fourth step never needs to be repeated.
- Maintenance inventory in step ten is spread out over time and is lighter than the one-time writing investment in step four.

3.2. Getting Ready

When we are ready to begin, we acquire:

- 5-10 **separate** single-subject spiral notebooks, college ruled.
- A few black pens.
- A quiet place to work.
- An hour a day (suggested).

The fourth step inventory is comprised of three inventories:

1. **The resentment inventory.**
2. **The fear inventory.**
3. **The sex inventory.**

4. Resentment Inventory

The resentment inventory requires three passes:

1. **Making the list.**
2. **Writing the cause and affects.**
3. **Writing the turnarounds.** (After praying for each party)

4.1. Making the List

In listing names:

Prepare the notebook(s).

- We take one of our fresh notebooks and write "Cause & Affects - Book 1" on the cover. This notebook will include both our list of names and our cause and affects.
- We may need more than one spiral notebook for our cause & affects. If so, we label the second book "Cause & Affects - Book 2", etc.
- We draw a vertical line down the center of the first page and any consecutive pages needed to complete our list. This allows two columns of names on each page.
- For the principles list we omit the divider line as the "names" are typically a bit longer.

We ask God for the list.

Real or imagined.

- We add names whether the offense was real or imagined.

Angry then or now.

- We add names that we are angry with now or *were* angry with in the past (even if the anger is not still active).

At this point we are only writing down names, we are not yet writing why we were angry.

4.1.1. People

We start with people.

List "People"

- At the top of the first page, we write "People" and circle it.

We get quiet and ask God to provide the list.

- Relex. We don't stress over forcing people or situations to come to mind.
- If we don't remember an offense, we move on. Remember, we are only listing names at this point (not the reason why we were angry).

Scan over our lives.

- Starting as far back as we can remember, we move forward one year (or phase) at a time until we reach the present.
- If we finish one session by getting up to the fifth grade for example, we know where to pick the next time we sit down to continue.

Types of names:

- We describe people if we can't remember their names: "kid with orange bike in grade 2", or "blonde girl in grade 5", or "manager at Acme restaurant", etc.
- We can include groups of people: "the Smith family", "the tennis team", or "sales staff at cable company", etc.

Number of names:

- It's common to have between 50-200 people listed, but of course it could be any number.

Leave a blank page for add-ons.

- When we're done with our people list, we leave a blank page for any people add-ons while working on institutions and principles.

4.1.2. Institutions

When we're done with people, we move on to institutions.

List "Institutions"

- Remember, leave one blank page for any people add-ons.
- Write "Institutions" on top of a new page and circle it.

We get quiet and ask God to provide the list.
Scan over our lives.

- Just like we did with people, we review our lives from beginning to present considering all the organizations and institutions with which we had been (or still are) angry.

Relax:

- Having invited God into this process, we relax and just list the names as they come to us - not avoiding any names, nor struggling to rack our brains - just smoothly listing the entities as they come to us.

Types of names:

- We list schools, teams, clubs, churches, religions, employers, businesses, corporations, industries, media outlets, governmental organizations, countries, collection agencies, hospitals, jails, gangs, etc.
- We list them either specifically or in general, as the case may be.

Number of names:

- Often there are between 15-30 names listed for institutions. But as always, this can vary widely.

Leave a blank page for add-ons.

- When we're done with institutions, we leave a blank page for any institutions add-ons while we move on to the principles list.

4.1.3. Principles

When we're done with institutions, we move on to principles.

List "Principles"

- Remember, leave one blank page for institutions add-ons.
- Write "Principles" on top of a new page and circle it.

We get quiet and ask God to provide the list.
Scan over our lives.

- Just like we did with institutions, we review our lives from beginning to present considering all the **principles** with which we had been (or still are) angry.

Relax:

- As with the other lists, we invite God into the process. We relax and list the ideas as they come to us - not struggling to rack our brains. Just smoothly listing them as they surface.
- This section can be a bit challenging and requires some patience.

Types of names:

- Principles can be a bit confusing to identify. Think of them as social expectations, social beliefs, ethics, rules, sayings, etc.
- Examples: "live and let live", "forgive frequently", "men should pay", "women should doll themselves up", "lying/stealing/cheating is wrong", "pull yourself up by your bootstraps", "rich/attractive people are more important than poor people", "poor people are freeloaders", "we get what we deserve", "let go, let God", "better to give than receive", "the sky's the limit", "the glass is half full/empty", "actions speak louder than words", "loners are losers", "reputation is everything", "sex outside of marriage is sinful", "only the strong survive", "the ends justify the means", etc.

Number of principles:

- A principles list often has between 15-30 items. Although, this too can vary widely.

4.1.4. Numbering List

When finished:

List any add-on names.

- We reflect and ask God to show us any further names to add to our people, institutions, and principles lists.

Number the names on all three lists.

- When we feel our lists are complete, we consecutively number all the items on our combined lists.
- We start at the first person in the "people" list and number straight through to the last principle.
- For example if our last person is number 150, then we number our first institution as number 151. And, if our last institution is number 175, then we make our first principle number 176.

4.1.5. Example List

People	
(1) Joe (2) Sam (3) Sue (4) Bully on kickball team (5) Jill ...	... (149) Sales staff at Acme company (150) Fred

Institutions	
(151) Acme elementary school (152) Anytown city government (153) Anytown police department (154) Acme corporation ...	... (173) Alcoholics Anonymous (174) This/that political party (175) Acme newspaper

Principles	
(176) Pull yourself up by your bootstraps (177) Ask for help (178) Chivalry (179) Competition is good (180) Embrace change ...	... (189) Tell the truth (190) An eye for an eye

Note: Numbering the items allows us to correspond the cause & affects with their associated turnarounds in a later notebook.

4.2. Writing the Cause and Affects

Review the Big Book example.

- The Big Book provides an example of how to write and organize both "the cause" and the "affects my" sections.
- Note how concise the examples are in the Big Book.

In this section we list:

- The number & name of the entity we resent.
- Why we have been angry; what did *they* do, or not do?
- Which of our instincts were threatened.
- And indicate that there is fear related to these resentments.

4.2.1. The Cause

Be concise.

- Remember how concise the examples are in the Big Book.
- We are not writing a novel, but rather documenting our fact-finding process.
- Again, inventory is not meant to provide mere self-knowledge. Rather, inventory provides the willingness to move from self-reliance to God-reliance once we see the shortcomings of a life based on self-will.

Why were we angry.

- We list the reasons why we have been angry with each person on our list.

4.2.2. Affects my

There are 7 instincts mentioned in the Big Book:

1. **Pride:** What I think others think of me.
2. **Self-esteem:** What I think of myself.
3. **Personal Relations:** My relationships with other people.
4. **Sex Relations:** My intimate relations. (Romantic, sexual. Real or imagined.)
5. **Ambitions:** What I want in my future.
6. **Pocketbook:** My financial resources and other assets.
7. **Security:** My sense of safety.

Note: These instincts are healthy when properly balanced, but when we feel they are threatened we can become excited, indulge in negativity, and respond poorly.

List threatened instincts.

- We list the instincts (from the 7 listed above) that we feel are threatened for each name on our list.

Indicate fear.

- Fear is not an instinct - instead fear is placed in parentheses (or circled) alongside our threatened instincts for each name on our list.
- When our instincts are threatened, we often get scared, which can then fuel our resentments.
- Indicating "fear" prepares us to look at our fears in the turnarounds section of the resentment inventory and then again further on in the fear inventory.

4.2.3. Example Cause and Affects

1. Joe
Cause: Stole my bike. Lied to my family. Gossiped about me.
Affects My: Security, pocketbook, self-esteem, pride. (fear)

2. Sam
Cause: He's rich and popular. Never paid me back. Made fun of me in front of others.
Affects My: Pocketbook, self-esteem, pride. (fear)

3. Sue
Cause: Likes Sam. Won't talk to me.
Affects My: Sex relations, ambitions, self-esteem, pride. (fear)

Note: The Big Book shows two basic approaches to writing cause and affects.

1. One method, illustrated by the Mr. Brown example, shows the listing out (indenting) of 3 distinct resentment items, each of which have their own list of affected instincts to their right.

2. A different type of example is seen in the "My wife" example, further down on that same page, which clumps all the resentment items together and then lists all the affected instincts together in the "affects my" column.

The later example, the "My wife" method, works efficiently and is shown in the examples above.

When we have worked through our entire list of people, institutions, and principles, we have then completed the cause & affects and are ready to move on to the turnarounds but first let's look at the resentment prayer.

4.3. The Resentment Prayer

As we arrive at each name while writing the turnarounds we pray the following (as indicated in the Big Book):

"God, help me realize that this person (or institution, or idea) is perhaps spiritually sick. Though I don't like their symptoms, they may be sick just like I have been. Please help me show them the same tolerance, pity, and patience that I would cheerfully grant a sick friend. How can I be helpful to them? Please save me from being angry. Thy will be done."

4.4. Writing the Turnarounds

Prepare the notebook(s).

- We start a fresh notebook and label it "Turnarounds - Book 1".
- If additional notebooks are needed we label them "Turnarounds - Book 2", etc.
- We place our "Cause & Affects - Book 1" on our left and open to our names-list.
- We place our new "Turnarounds - Book 1" notebook on our right.

Recite the resentment prayer.

- With the first name in mind, we state the resentment prayer as indicated above.
- We continue this for each name on our list as we come to them.

Answer the turnaround questions.

- For each name on our list, we write the answers to the following turnaround questions (in our new turnarounds notebook):

  - **Where was I selfish?**
  - **Where was I dishonest?**
  - **Where was I self-seeking?**
  - **Where was I frightened?**

Note:
- **By writing ALL of our outward behaviors in the <u>self-seeking question</u> of the turnarounds, we can then use that section as our core 8th step amends list.**
- **Remember, we make amends for our behaviors and omissions of responsibilities, not our thoughts.**

4.4.1. Selfish

We answer this question: **Where was I selfish?**

Selfish *thinking*.

- We write down how our <u>thinking</u> was overly focused on ourselves to the disregard, disrespect, and detriment of other people.

Save *behaviors* for self-seeking section.

- We save any selfish <u>behaviors</u> for the self-seeking section of our turnarounds because those outward behaviors will be part of our amends list.

Templates for the selfish question:

- "I was more concerned about getting what I wanted and disregarded them (in this way - fill in the blank)."
- Example: I was more concerned about getting attention through gossiping about others and sarcasm that I disregarded their standing and reputation in the community.
- "I wished them harm instead of praying for them, forgiving them, and turning them over to God."

4.4.2. Dishonest

We answer this question: **Where was I dishonest?**

Self-deception.

- We write down our self-deception; the lies we tell ourselves.

Save behaviors for the self-seeking section.

- Again, we save any dishonest <u>behaviors</u> for the self-seeking section of our turnarounds because those outward behaviors will be part of our amends list.

Templates for the dishonest question:

- "I told myself (state the unfounded assumption or belief here) when actually (state what is closer to the truth here)."
- Example: I told myself that their opinion and treatment of me indicated my value, when actually God loves and values me unconditionally.
- I told myself that they deserved negative consequences when actually it is not my place to judge and condemn God's children.
- I told myself that they are unimportant, when actually God values all of us equally.

4.4.3. Self-seeking

We answer this question: **Where was I self-seeking?**

List behaviors.

- This is the key section where we list all of our outward <u>behaviors</u>.
- This allows us to have a one-stop location for our core amends list in step 8.

List offenses.

- Any stealing, cheating, and lying - even though these are dishonest behaviors, we place them here for our amends list.
- Any of our physical or verbal behaviors of retaliation, cruelty, gossip/character-assassination, etc. toward others.
- Any omissions of our responsibilities as a child, parent, friend, partner, employee / employer, citizen, etc..

4.4.4. Frightened

We answer this question: **Where was I frightened?**

List fears.

- This is where we indicate fears we have that are related to the name are writing about.

Template for the frightened question:

- "I was/am afraid that…".
- Example: "I was afraid that if I remained quiet that I would just blend in and nobody would ever notice me, that I would be left behind."

4.4.5. Example Turnarounds

1. Joe

Selfish (S): I wanted to parade around with my new bike so that the neighborhood would think I was really special. I have resented him for decades instead of keeping it in context and praying for him.

Dishonest (D): I told myself that he gossiped about me, when I don't know that for sure.

Self-seeking (SS): I gossiped about him every chance I got. I damaged his bike in retaliation.

Frightened (F): That my possessions aren't safe. That I'm unworthy of respect. That everyone wants to make fun of me and undermine me.

2. Sam

S: I only wanted good things to happen to me. I didn't want anyone to be more comfortable or happier than me. I wished him harm instead of seeing him as a child of God.

D: I told myself that if I wasn't receiving the gifts that others were experiencing that God must not love me, when actually God loves us all equally and I was blocking my own happiness in life. I conveniently disregarded the fact that I had told Sam that he didn't have to pay me back.

SS: My negativity and self-pity has kept me from being present for God and others. I told people that Sam was a cheapskate.

F: That I'm unworthy of friends, comfort, and God's blessings.

3. Sue

S: I didn't want her to like anyone but me. I expected her to know I wanted to be her boyfriend.

D: I told myself that I was unattractive because Sue didn't pay attention to me, when actually as God's creation I am beautiful and loved. I told myself Sue wouldn't talk to me, when actually I never even tried to start a conversation with her.

SS: I made up lies about her to my friends and used mean names when talking about her. I indulged in negativity and remained unavailable for God and others.

F: That I'm unattractive and unworthy of sex & love.

5. Fear Inventory

The fear inventory requires two passes:

1. **Making the list.**
2. **Writing the fears.**

5.1. Making the List

Prepare our notebooks.

- We take our our notebook titled "Turnarounds - Book 1" and place it in front of us on our left.
- We take out another fresh notebook and write "Fear Inventory" on the cover - we place this notebook in front of us to the right.

Fears from our turnarounds.

- We go through the frightened section of our turnarounds (the notebook on our left) and transfer all those fears into a draft-list fears in our new "Fear Inventory" notebook on our right.
- Then we go back through our draft-list (making a new, clean list) consolidating any redundant fears so that we have gleaned a complete list of unique fears.
- We do this with all our our turnarounds notebooks (if we have more than one).

Add fears not connected with resentments.

- Next, we add on any other fears which did not have any resentments connected to them.
- Examples: "snakes", "wild animals", "car crashes", "epidemics", "tornadoes", "unexpected events", etc.

5.2. Writing the Fears

Skip a page.

- We skip a page after our fear list in our "Fear Inventory" notebook and answer the following questions for each item in our fear list:

"Fear:"

- We write down the first fear indicated on our list.

"Why:"

- We write down our first experience of that fear and any other major experience of that fear in our lives.

"Self-reliance fails:"

- We write how we attempted to manage this fear and that how the result of these attempts failed (based on our finite selves). [Note: When we are not connected to God, self-reliance always fails, if we look closely enough.]
- Example: "I tried to be everyone's friend, doing everything I could for them so that they would all like me, the result was that people found me fakey and irritating, I became exhausted, and even more depressed."

"Trusting and relying on God..."

- We write **"Trusting and relying on infinite loving God would allow me to...(fill in the blank)."**
- We fill in the blank with what we imagine God could do for us in the context of removing that fear; what we could experience if we were filled with courage and love.
- Example: "Trusting and relying on infinite loving God would allow me to relax. I would be able to be comfortable around others, have fun, and be authentically helpful when appropriate."

"God please remove my fear..."

- Lastly, we write **"God, please remove my fear of (fill in the blank here by listing the fear again) and turn my attention to what you would have me be."**
- This is a prayer and is written and read in that spirit.

5.3. Example Fear Inventory

Fear: That my possessions aren't safe.

Why: My bike was stolen when I was in grade school. My car was broken into a few years ago.

Self-reliance fails: Sometimes I didn't buy nice things because I've been afraid they will get stolen, the result was I remained in fear and didn't get the enjoyment of quality products. I didn't have people over to visit so that they wouldn't know what I own, the result was that this severely limited my social life.

Trusting and relying on infinite loving God would allow me to: relax. I would know that whatever God wants me to have, enjoy, and share will be provided for me through reasonable efforts. I could comfortably acquire quality belongings, enjoying them and sharing them in a reasonable and thoughtful manner. I would take reasonable steps to secure my belongings. I would not suffer from worry or paranoia over my belongings being damaged or stolen - this would allow me to be present in my life, for God, and others.

God, please remove my fear that my possessions aren't safe **and turn my attention to what you would have me be.**

Fear: That I'm unworthy of respect.

Why: Kids made fun of me on the playground. I spent time in jail.

Self-reliance fails: I have made fun of other people in retribution, the result was that this damaged my social life. I tried to act more important than others, the result was that this feeling was short-lived and left me depressed - also people found me arrogant and avoided me. I pretended I didn't care what other people thought of me, the result was that inside I was actually still obsessed about getting people to think highly of me and then I lost touch with my own feelings.

Trusting and relying on infinite loving God would allow me to: relax. I would get my sense of dignity directly from the love of God. My self-respect would be independent of what people thought of me. With this confidence, I could move forward in my life, engaging with other people comfortably and respectfully.

God, please remove my fear that I'm unworthy of respect **and turn my attention to what you would have me be.**

6. Sex Inventory

The sex inventory is the last part in the inventory process.

Ask for God's help.

- We ask God to be with us in this work.

Focus on manipulation to get sex.

- Although it is possible that information about specific sex acts may enter into the writing of the sex inventory, the vast majority of the writing in this section is about how we thought and behaved in selfish ways as we attempted to manipulate other people around us.

Further additions to 8th step amends list.

- Note: When we arrive at step 8, we will not only take from the "self-seeking" portion of the resentment inventory turnarounds section, but also from this sex inventory where offensive behaviors may show up in answers to the various questions.

6.1. Making the List

Prepare the notebook(s).

- We take out a fresh notebook and title it "Sex Inventory".

Make a list.

- We start out the sex inventory by making a list of names.
- These include people from our past and present.
- People with whom we had sexual, romantic, or intimate experiences.
- It also can include people whom we were obsessive in our imagination.
- Our list can include items like pornography, prostitution, bath houses, etc.
- If we can't remember a person's name, we can use a descriptor, such as "one-night stand at acme bar", etc.

6.2. Written Work

Once we have our list, we answer the following nine questions for each name on our list:

- **Where was I selfish?** We look for where we were we focused on ourselves to the detriment of other(s).

- **Where was I dishonest?** We look for where we failed to keep our commitments, where did we lie, misrepresent, or exaggerate, etc.

- **Where was I inconsiderate?** We look for where we failed to consider our affect on other people or failed in our responsibilities.

- **Whom had I hurt?** This can include the person with whom we may have shared intimacy and other affected people: family, friends, other partners, etc.

- **Where did I unjustifiably arouse jealousy?** We look for where we intentionally or carelessly caused another person to experience jealousy. Maybe we intentionally caused jealousy in an attempt to manipulate someone's perception of us.

- **Where did I unjustifiably arouse suspicion?** We look for where we intentionally or carelessly caused another person to experience suspicion. Maybe we intentionally caused suspicion to gain attention.

- **Where did I unjustifiably arouse bitterness?** We look for where we intentionally or carelessly caused another person to experience bitterness. Maybe we intentionally caused bitterness as a form of retribution or to feel powerful.

- **Where was I at fault?** For this question we add any other offenses and harm we created beyond what has been answered in the previous questions.

- **What should I have done instead?** With the principles of kindness, love, tolerance, and honesty in mind, we write down what would have been appropriate behavior.

6.3. Example Sex Inventory

Name: Jane Doe (affair)

Where was I selfish? I wanted immediate pleasure without caring how others might be affected. I wanted my friends to be impressed that I took her home.

Where was I dishonest? I had previously promised to my partner that I would be faithful but I broke that promise. I told myself that if my partner didn't find out, that it didn't matter, when actually I needed to honor my commitments regardless of who was aware of my behavior.

Where was I inconsiderate? I didn't discuss safe sex or use protection, thus risking the possibility of bringing a communicative disease back to my partner. I didn't consider that Jane Doe might get pregnant - I assumed if she did, that she would get an abortion.

Whom had I hurt? My flagrant disregard for Jane Doe's wellbeing and dignity hurt her. I damaged the quality of my relationship with my partner. I risked the health of Jane Doe, my partner, and myself. I affected my partner's relationships with her friends and family when we eventually broke up over this act of infidelity. I let down people who had formerly seen me as a role model.

Where did I unjustifiably arouse jealousy? When I ran into Jane Doe at the grocery store (with my partner) I flirted and laughed with Jane Doe, thinking that my partner would see me as more desirable.

Where did I unjustifiably arouse suspicion? By acting macho in front of my friends when I took Jane Doe home, they started to call me "the charmer" in front of my partner - my partner asked me why they had started to call me that name.

Where did I unjustifiably arouse bitterness? I caused hurt and bitterness in my partner, her friends, and family when we broke up because of this. I hurt Jane Doe as she was hoping that our intimacy was going to turn into something - her friends were upset with me when they found out about my selfish and misleading conduct.

Where was I at fault? I broke my commitment to my partner, I was selfish and inconsiderate. I risked the health of Jane Doe, my partner, myself, and any of our future partners that might also have been affected. I was unthinking, inconsiderate, and used people to aggrandize my status and sense of self.

What should I have done instead? Instead, I should have honored my commitment to my partner. I shouldn't have flirted with Jane Doe, nor gone home with her. I should have gotten my sense of value from my relationship with God so that I wouldn't have felt the need to show off in front of other people, or use people to feel powerful. Even though I shouldn't have even been with Jane Doe, I should have practiced safe sex.

6.4. Sane & Sound Sex Ideal

Create our sane & sound sex ideal.

- When we are finished writing our sex inventory, we review it and consider what we have found.
- Using this information, keeping in mind the concepts of consideration, honesty, and love, we write down our target **sane and sound sex ideal**.
- This is our core sex ideal to work toward.
- This ideal may continue to evolve over time.

7. Step Five Reading

7.1. Preparing for Reading

The writing in step four provides us with four basic sections of writing:

- **Resentment inventory cause & affects.**
- **Resentment inventory turnarounds.**
- **Fear inventory.**
- **Sex inventory (including our sane & sound sex ideal).**

7.2. Reading Step Five

We get together with our sponsor or other trusted person, following the guidelines and suggestions in the Big Book, to conduct our fifth step.

When we are ready, we take out our notebooks and read exactly what we have written in our fourth step inventory to this witness.

Reading the resentment inventory:

- We start by placing our Cause & Affects notebook in front of us on the left and open it to our number one entry.

- We simultaneously place our Turnarounds notebook in front of us on the right and likewise open it to the first entry.

- We begin by reading the Cause & Affects for "person-one" in our notebook on our left , and then read the corresponding material for that same person in the Turnarounds notebook on our right.

- Sample reading style: "I resent Joe. Cause: Stole my bike. Lied to my family. Gossiped about me. Affects my: Security, pocketbook, self-esteem, pride, *and there is fear*. Selfish: I wanted to parade around with my new bike...etc." (See sample layout below).

7.3. Example Reading Layout for Cause & Affects / Turnarounds

Cause & Affects Notebook   Turnarounds Notebook

1. Joe
Cause: Stole my bike. Lied to my
family. Gossiped about me.
Affects My: Security, pocketbook,
self-esteem, pride. (fear)

2. Sam
Cause: He's rich and popular. Never
paid me back. Made fun of me in front
of others.
Affects My: Pocketbook, self-esteem,
pride. (fear)

3. Sue
Cause: Likes Sam. Won't talk to me.
Affects My: Sex relations, ambitions,
self-esteem, pride. (fear)

---

1. Joe
Selfish (S): I wanted to parade around with my new bike
so that the neighborhood would think I was really special.
I have resented him for decades instead of keeping it in
context and praying for him.
Dishonest (D): I told myself that he gossiped about me,
when I don't know that for sure.
Self-seeking (SS): I gossiped about him every chance I
got. I damaged his bike in retaliation.
Frightened (F): That my possessions aren't safe. That I'm
unworthy of respect. That everyone wants to make fun of
me and undermine me.

2. Sam
S: I only wanted good things to happen to me. I didn't want
anyone to be more comfortable or happier than me. I wished
him harm instead of seeing him as a child of God.
D: I told myself that if I wasn't receiving the gifts that others
were experiencing that God must not love me, when actually
God loves us all equally and I was blocking my own
happiness in life. I conveniently disregarded the fact that I had
told Sam that he didn't have to pay me back.
SS: My negativity and self-pity has kept me from being
present for God and others. I told people that Sam was a
cheapskate.
F: That I'm unworthy of friends, comfort, and God's blessings.

3. Sue
S: I didn't want her to like anyone but me. I expected her to
know I wanted to be her boyfriend.
D: I told myself that I was unattractive because Sue didn't pay
attention to me, when actually as God's creation I am
beautiful and loved. I told myself Sue wouldn't talk to me,
when actually I never even tried to start a conversation with
her.
SS: I made up lies about her to my friends and used mean
names when talking about her. I indulged in negativity and
remained unavailable for God and others.
F: That I'm unattractive and unworthy of sex & love.

We continue reading the cause & affects / turnarounds.

- After we have read the cause & affects and turnarounds for "person-one" as described above, we move on to "person-two".
- We read the cause & affects for "person-two" in the left notebook, followed by the turnarounds for "person-two" in the right notebook.
- We continue this process through our entire resentment list.

We then read our fear inventory.

Finally we read our sex inventory (and chosen ideal).

At the end, it often proves beneficial to then take the opportunity to share anything else we feel is burdensome, getting these items off our chest, even if something did not show up in any of the inventory work.

8. Step Eight Amends List

When we arrive at step eight we review the self-seeking section in our resentment inventory turnarounds and the material in our sex inventory. We add on any other amends we know of to create our complete amends list, asking God for help with this process.

9. Step Ten Inventory

<u>Continue written inventory</u>

We continue the written inventory process that we learned in step four.

When troubled.

- When we are troubled (even after prayer or talking with another person) we get out our 10th step notebook and write the appropriate inventory entry.
- When we finish the writing, we call our sponsor or trusted person and read it.
- We then make necessary amends.

<u>10th Step Writing</u>

There are 3 types of entries in written tenth step inventory:

1. **Resentment inventory entry includes:**

   a. Cause & affects.
   b. Immediately followed by turnarounds.
   c. Then we roll right from the *frightened* section of the turnarounds into a fear inventory and process all the fear inventory questions.

2. **Fear inventory entry:**

   We process fears exactly as we did in step four.

3. **Sex inventory entry:**

   We process a sex inventory entry exactly as we did in step four.

9.1. Example 10th Step Resentment Inventory

Resent: Jill

Cause: She didn't show up to watch the kids as she had promised, I missed my plane.

Affects: Pocketbook, ambitions, personal relations (fear).

Selfish: I expected her to be reliable instead of taking responsibility to get proper references.

Dishonest: I told myself it was her fault that I missed my plane when actually I should have backup plans when I have important dates to keep.

Self-seeking: I have indulged in negativity over this for three full days instead of learning from it, praying for her, and moving on.

Frightened: That I will lose my job. That others will see me as incapable and irresponsible.

Why (did I have this fear / when did I originally experience this fear): I missed the field trip bus in second grade, got called into the principal's office, and was made fun of by other kids.

Self-reliance fails: I imagine what I could say to Jill to make her feel guilty and ashamed, but this keeps me feeling negative and self-righteous and then I can't let It go. I try to over-apologize to my work colleagues, but they experience my repeated apologies as an opportunity to complain about the babysitter. I try beating up on myself in hopes that I will never again make any mistakes but then I lose energy and get depressed.

Trusting and relying on infinite loving God would allow me to: relax. I could learn from this experience and have a backup babysitter when I have to go out of town for business. I could see that everything happens for a reason and that I actually was able to stay home and console my sister who lost her husband a week ago. I would gain compassion for other people when things appear to go wrong in their lives.

God please remove my fear that I will lose my job and that others will see me as incapable and irresponsible **and turn my attention to what you would have me be.**

10. Helping Others

We begin to enjoy the flow of God's grace in our lives and our attention turns to helping others in step 12.

If we have done a thorough job of the work laid out in the Big Book as detailed here in this guidebook, we can confidently show another person how to do this work.

Seeing others experience serenity and God as a result of this work is a wonderful affirming experience. We then feel ourselves a valuable part of God's world.

The people we work with are then able to pass on clear directions to others.

Alcoholism & Addiction AA Recovery Handbook

How To Write A Fourth Step As The Key To Recovery For The Alcoholic & Addict

Copies available on www.amazon.com

Made in the USA
Las Vegas, NV
17 February 2024

85898780R00026